Karmic Soup

By Keitha B

Copyright©2017 Keitha B Cole. All rights reserved.
ISBN 978-1-365-97817-3

Cover Art: Ari Rowan

To my loving fans, especially those I call family.

-Keitha B

Table of Contents:

The Warnings:

Forward………………………………………………….7

Message…………………………………………………..8

'Spective………………………………………………...10

Silent Commodity……………………………………….11

What a Hipster Can't Hear……………………………...13

Grandmother…………………………………………….14

A Wind's Advice………………………………………...15

Diet………………………………………………………16

Edgewater……………………………………………….17

The Journey:

A Song's Portrait………………………………………...19

Pearl……………………………………………………...20

The Now Blossom……………………………………….21

Tuesday………………………………………………….22

Painter vs. Muse…………………………………………23

Bargain Hunter…………………………………………..24

Commodity..26

Suture..27

Dance's Portrait...28

Denouement:

Where to Go...31

Adored...32

Calico..33

Forecast...34

Tell Me..36

To Addiction, Love KB..............................37

Heroes...38

Roundabout...39

Bennett Christmas.....................................41

The Love of the Classic............................42

The Warnings

Forward

The wind, it whispers a song, my friend.

To this you must listen and apply.

The shouts and screams from about you can be so loud, so easily brought to your ears.

DON'T LISTEN.

The whisper on the wind carries the strength the shout forgot.

Message

I waited for the message,
Waited in my car as the meter ran down.
I waited,
Contemplating what happens to meters
If no one is there to rhythmically challenge them.
I waited and,
As I pictured time imploding,
Someone screamed, "Beat's not dead!"

And I sat there waiting for the message, thinking,
"Was it sleeping?
Is time the essence?
What awaits us at the gates?"
I sat there waiting for the message
Not knowing what to anticipate.
All good meters do time;
And time like any other dimension can opt to rhyme.

The meter ran down.

So, I started my car,
Fixated on the cadence of people walking out a jazz quintet,
The spontaneous glances
Of eyes locking and unlocking,
The possibility of future after future…
A dance of oncoming traffic
That voice again,
"Beat's not dead."

I sat at a red light
Waiting for the message,
Hoping it could find me where I could park for free.
I fell asleep with my eyes open
And that voice again
"Beat's not dead"
Was it all in my head?
The message? The meter? Is time of the essence?
These questions like beacons to a place to park.

'Spective

Poets stand in line to explain it,
Though their lives attempt to evade it when diving for deeper truths.
But life shorts no one of the reality,
Merely an angle or two.

Silent Commodity

Why does any smile have to end?
Why silent worlds where there is not one friend?
Just thieves and liars
And knives that won't bend;
Just thieves and liars
And voices in one's head.

And no one can care
If they can't hear what you've said.

But my mouth won't move
And I'm losing at this game.
Love is too hard to prove
When no one knows my name.
Just peers and beggars
And dreams of having more;
Just peers and beggars
With no settling the score.

And no one can care
If they can't hear what you've said.
I sing and I sing
And I go home to bed.
I am two dimensional chasms
With the weary, as I dread,
Nightmares of the man and woman fighting
As I fled.
In the stairwell, she is crying,
And her face hurts my head

I think, "No one cares,"
But I heard what was said.
I am quiet, in a panic,

But I go home to bed
I am two dimensional chasms…

She is sparkling, charming jewels

That aren't fed…

Just forged by the force of being buried.

I don't know whether to fight to feel
Or fight to feel numb.

What a Hipster Can't Hear

Locked down
On a river stretch,
I thought I had lost what I hadn't gained yet.

I shouted,
    Unclouded.
        It was loud,
            Unfound,
                Like a rock
            Who's gained its gravity
            I sank
                Out of sound.

What did I see?
No sound means no light,
Trapped in a silence that drowns you
Outright.

Don't forget while it soaks through your bones…
Why you're livin on the surface
Trying to get higher.

Grandmother

She told us that we "suffer for our beauty"
But when grandmother comes home...
A wonderful thing happens.

When grandmother comes home,
The softest of voices echoes through the halls
Some amazing confidence makes me feel tall
When grandmother comes home.

When grandmother comes home there is a story or another
I encapture another country
Another culture
Another dish.
When grandmother comes home I learn about the mystery
I learn about the history
The movies and books

I look on to what a strong woman must have took
And with such grace
And how strong
I know as her daughters sing along.
Grandmother passed on that gracious poise
There is glamour with that strength
A quiet glamour,
Effortless and without clamor...
Just a beautiful, beautiful woman
Who seems never to have suffered
But must have very much!

A Wind's Advice

When love tries,
Failing to reach your ears,
But wrenching your heart with every word,
Remember,
That your time is yours and what you make of it;
That without wings you cannot fly off this hill;
That some just know what they need to fulfill
And some see it clearer
By falling to the bottom
And looking up.

Diet

It's a "blip" on the screen of life.
It's like rodeos for ravers,
Or selling Swatches for shoe salesmen.
It's like making your mind up
    And that time between being served and when you order,
  A little regret because you're going for the salad and not the steak.

But it's time:

Time to stop begging for life to treat you fairly,
Time to tell it like it is,
Because
it's
so unusual.
It's like answering your phone to a dial tone and trying not to hear your neighbors conversation.
It's like meandering to sit.
It's that temple inside where you practice pushing past the pain…
It's that time again.

Edgewater

wake me when the now comes
to the silent ashen embers of a night fire
to the memories of dancing and laughter
to the world not daring whispers
filling my peripheries

wake me when the now comes
to the rhythm of the morning down a path of sunlit dew
to the factory of nature balancing against my polluting clan

wake me to the limits of our existence
to the joy that fills me with hope
to the morning
the beginning
after the change

The Journey

A Song's Portrait

She gets that picture in her head.
She gets that picture,
And it's not in vain,
That image that keeps her sane.

She reaches that epiphany.
She crawls to that height.
She reaches enthralled
By the taste of her own might.

She sings with passion
Describing that picture.
She reaches that epiphany of sound
so right to describe it,
    That picture of the light.
As if no one else could say it she sings it,
Weaving imaginations with it:
That picture.

And imagine that future!
Light uniting us all.
Those nights where darkness can't win,
    Days of imaginings that everybody's in…
    The future
    But restless
        To be one with that picture,
           That song
        Revealed to the mind,
           And with epiphany
                Combined.

Pearl

There is no other wax
Than a friend.

There is no other way
Than to be,
And to be wisely…

To be one
Contained,

To know value
Within.

Without this
We are fever.

Without justice
We are existence
Without life.

We are plain
Outside

Until we are sacred.

The Now Blossom

The fiery flower
That lit up my dreary day
Says peaceful things
That carry me to a place of time standing still.

The flower's scent,
Distinct,
Threatening of chaos,
Somehow knows a way or two through my mind's own fury.
I breathe it in and my heart quiets.

Fiery flower,
Whose beauty challenges the height of the trees,
You stand in the field
And remind me to look around, that beauty is everywhere.

Tuesday

We gathered up all the things meant for the birds and fed them to the phoenix in the back yard. Dog bones flew from the earth as we all split the scene. I remember my homegirl saying she felt like plot shrapnel as the guys carried on about some girl in graphic detail.

   We were soon soothed, like dreads-R-us exploded, and we faded into the clouds like a broken halo on dead-lot screaming –

"BOO YAH"… I am rocked awake as Rita pulls in to Tower City. The Cavs won again. I am full of Love, heart pounding from culture shock; eyes fluttering not to look into eyes; everyone is beautiful.

   Overwhelmed, I push past the crowds of people, wondering how we're chosen to reside. I hear a voice say, "Like truth is a pendulum, my child, and love the vertigo high to one side."

My heart is swollen, one miracle after another. No friendly devils, no pipers to speak of, freedom proving to be freedom.
No heartless laws to force the masses into placid contraction-
just a rhythm of growth into joy into bearing hardship for more joy.

   I walk around an old white wino mumbling about mustard and shame and apples, "like one mistake began and ended everything that is beautiful," he says, chasing down a hotdog with a partially revealed bottle of Woodchuck.

   I wonder if he is homeless, and where his phoenix flies.

Painter vs. Muse

It's a battle, she seemed to imply.
Her brush strokes on the canvas in front of her in lieu of sobs...
Her adversary
The canvas itself
Was wrought with him
And his lust for the secret of her pain

But her gun,
her brush,
her smile
went untouched
protected
..... by her passion not to shoot
.....by her strokes on the canvas
......by her refusal to hide her eyes

Bargain Hunter

There's no toss up.
I am piecing together the past,
The race to integrity coagulating my senses:
Another teacher is speaking of Love within;
Another number of sparks lighting up the human grid.
I am tempting the night with offers of praise
And prayers for the whole human race,
Wondering if
Another oppressor is planning
Another impossible-to-ignore destruction of human dignity.
The rhythm of the repetition batters my mind
      I look up from my computer as I am beamed
through time:
              Just another medium day
              Of medium pain
              And medium rain.

 I am piecing together the past,
Seeking the moment when all was lost.
I tempt the night with offering of prayer.
I dread the velocity of others' torment passing;
Our wildest dreams of a better love a-massing-
How much do the tormented notice the rain?

The news
I am collecting,
Gathering information on what formation my Nation is
taking.
A dirty politician digs up bones of another

Another baby is born
Who sets her eyes on the love of a father
Whose dying wish will be her happiness
       I look up at the clock as it refuses to chime:
            Just another digital grail
            That will never fail
            Until magnetic hail.

There's no toss up.
I am piecing together the past,
Racing and coagulating, seeking the moment.
I am tempting the night with offers of praise
With prayers for my clique to honor another;
With prayers for impossible-to-ignore mercy;
With prayers for Love loving Love.
I try to remember
There is a light in us all,
Contagious,
Reeking of truth and humanity.

Commodity

Beauty
Outrageously conformed
To a state below humility
There's a difference
Between servitude
And slavery accepted

Beauty
Wasted on my flesh
I long to lift above the pain
There's a difference
Between a friend
And a partner in popularity

Cold
In my bones
From beauty
Imbedded in my fragile province
My army resorting
      To coveting angels

<u>Suture</u>

I visualize everything,
    Like everything is
        Burning heart,
        Healing eyes,
        Mending soul…
    Like time is built with thread.
  I reach in
    To a different space,
      Unable to feel my old depth,
        It feels shallow.
That which damages me
 Calls out to reconcile
   Like you could replace the lives that were to go,
      And you can make the nights stop coming,
        And the rain,
          And the snow…
      And hurricanes don't matter.
    But trees don't have guns!
  I run,
    Even still,
Like a bear is chasing me….
  I run and I run
Air not getting to my lungs
   So, I am caught
     And his claw is through my ribs

    Can I breathe in through that space?

I visualize everything,
  Like everything is
    Burning heart,
    Healing eyes,
    Mending soul,
  Like time is built with thread.

Dance's Portrait

She gets that picture in her head
And it's not in vain.
She gets that message,
That answer,
Like the sunlight through the rain.

She dances as if speaking,
Breath transcends the pain.
Her motion
Is her message
Like the wind through sunlit rain.

Denouement

A cold wind
An indestructible sound mocking silence
I reach with both hands through the howls
To embrace,
*   To replace,*
*   The pressure on my face*
And reduce the sting.
                              -Keitha B.

Where to Go

I knew not where to go from here…
the wreckage from that awesome fear,
from the game we have become…
      How inertia fades to dying,
No one now inside lies crying.

Words of forgiveness,
The standing of beating hearts, and falling of rescue tears
Are the groove of persistence;
Are the light of ascension;
Are the Mother and Father,
Friends again.

Adored

I feel like a dying whale.
A thousand fish cling to my tail.
A rainbow is not smiling above me.
How much of this world really loved me?

All of that mattered a second ago…
But I am soaring now!
Push on my wings and I go a bit higher.
    Spread and grow,
        Gaining speed,
            With the wind I will float
                Over trees
                    And the sea
                        And a boat!
                              Harpoons flying

                            A whale
                                tossing…

<u>calico</u>

But the trees are turning and so must I…
What beauty lies below the sky on the horizon as I look
over the forest that sits in the valley.
The hills here aren't as tall as the ones back home.
No one but me in this poem.
So I lie below the sky, changing colors with the passing of
the sun.
The light mingling with my yellows and oranges,
I am one big collage, a calico, spreading my paws along the
floor for a stretch.
Parts of me come together.
Everything comes together.
This is what's missing.
I will watch as the sun goes down over the leaves.
I will watch with a keen eye.
I will watch the house go dark
Alone in the poem.

Forecast

None but a word could afford
That crazy genius of
                                  Relaxed
                     Human
            Vibrato
       There is mellow-tone
       There is funkadilee
       There is crescendo
There is a time in space
There is space in that place
Where you've never been
               And in time
    In that place
  There is a smile
And that smile plays music in your style
               There is music every mile
                   In your walk
                   In your talk
        In that boogie freestyle razzmatazz
        The sequence of frequent
        You, me and we style
        Heartfelt Jazz

                There is mellow-tone
                There is Motown
                There is crescendo
       There is a peace of mind
       There is a mind at peace
       With family
       With friends

          With dividends
There is a rhythm
  There is future
There is much less ache
   It's just the words
There in the crazy genius of
                        Relaxed
                                  Human
                                            Vibrato
        There is mellow-tone
        There is music
        There is crescendo
There are a million heartbeats
Pounding out the way
Like rain pouring down after a drought

Tell Me

Clouded
But before I
Bumble away
Tell me to stay
Tell me to be here with you
Tell me it isn't the money
Tell me insecure's not funny
Tell me again
In no words
The way Love tells you

Before I contemplate goodbye
And look up, afraid
Into your eyes
Tell me there's something more to do
Tell me you hate to see me cry
The way Love tells you

Before I try to sneak away
Overwhelmed by the kindness you have displayed
Tell me to chill
The way you do
Without a word
Say I'm not a fool
As if Love tells you

To Addiction: Love, My Higher Self

You're drifting out of my life and I'm happy for myself.
You are an echo of a thought,
Lost in the dying groove of the habitual mind.
You search and search for a way back into my life.

Alas, I do not think you have a place here.
I'm moving on, now,
To better things.
I am tempted by the wheel of new beginnings
And you will not stop me.

Heroes

You see their toys,
Mountains-
No, volcanoes- spilling out of the box onto the floor.
You wonder if they could possibly get bored.
And if they get bored,
What next?
What way would they tie the curtains on to save the world?

Roundabout

It was here that I left you
You were not withered.
You had a sharpness,
Not like thorns
But like light.
You gifted me with a quest to find you again from darkness.
You promised your return, and yet it is I returning.
Hello Self!
You monstrosity!
You beaten path to
Love internal…

Together we will mend the fences
Tawny treescape, like a painting,
Yet a shield of earthy self-care…

It will be our space.
We will free ourself in the mire of solitude,
Break the ice of isolation so that touching lives will be good again…
Good like the mornings that used to come
As if one with each sunrise.

We will break the habits
And use them for kindling.
The healing rising from the flames
Into the atmosphere-
Round membranous facsimile of the sphere our body romps on.

There was no peace in the darkness.
Medals, prizes of anguish,
For which I died again and again,

Clinking around my skeleton as I amassed a protective
coating on my outsides.

Eve would be proud to know that I have found Eden here
within you, me…
You piece of God,
You brilliant light.

It is with you that I seek *comfort*
That thing that scares me with privilege
When it is really a right that no one can truly share, only
hope for one another.

So we've turned a page, you and I.
Completed a circle…
Or was it a cheating symbol of a star
That crosses its own path
Several eternal times…

If only to be with you
Like this:
Contained in an endless snuggle of rejuvenation and
wonder
So that when I die again, it is peaceful…
With you…
To you…
For you…
From you, yet never leaving

Bennett Christmas

The children move to the rhythm of peace.
The mothers' freedom starts to increase.
The fathers love;
The uncles, too;
The aunts and grandmas: their hullabaloo.
And grandpa sits quietly
Humming a tune
That sounds like the ocean
Under the moon.

The Love of the Classic

Time is timeless with you
Where we begin and end is gone
Only we remain
All complexity is missing
Each step is another eternity
Where Love rules

Poet's Afterward

If you're reading this, you either know me or want to get to know me a little better. All I can say is it indeed has been a journey. These last seven years have not been prolific in the least. Most of this poetry was written between 1997 and 2009. In the hopes that reading and typing it up would help my budding relationship with writing again, I've put this together for people to read. I also hoped that the stuff that touched the lives of those that heard it would be more readily available for more people to read. I am unaccustomed to sharing with a faceless audience. But I suppose a poet can't meet all her fans face-to-face. So, until we meet, if we meet....Thanks for reading!